NICE TO BE WITH YOU AGAIN!

A Star Original

More humour from the two irrepressible
Ronnies:

Today in the courts an unemployed labourer
was found guilty of running up and down
Downing St at two o'clock in the morning
shouting 'All the government is barmy!'
He was given a two pound fine for being drunk
and disorderly and a ten-year gaol sentence for
revealing a state secret.

A journalist who slandered the Chancellor of
the Exchequer very badly was given a chance
to do better in the High Court today.

And at the Old Bailey, Jim Spraggs, the
world's greatest confidence trickster, sentenced
the Judge to five years' hard labour.

D0596947

All the news items in this book are real and not made up at all. However if they *had* been they'd have been written by:
Peter Bain, Robert Belford, Peter Campbell, Garry Chambers, Barry Cryer, Manny Curtis, Tommy Desmond, M. H. Drew, Dave Dutton, Stan Edwards, Harry Evans, Derek Farmer, Ernest Forbes, Tony Hare, Tony Hawes, Les Higgins, Tudor Jones, Dorothy Kilmurry-Hall, Frank Kirkbride, Gary Knight, Les Lilley, Ray Lowry, Malcolm Mather, Tony Mather, Wally Malston, David McKellar, Tom Magee-Englefield, Philip Munnoch, David Nobbs, Gavin Osbon, Tony Payne, Terry Ravenscroft, Tony Rich, Peter Robinson, Neil Shand, Austin Steele, Edward Taylor, Dick Vosburgh, David Webb, Ron Weighell and Gerald Wiley.

Also featuring the Two Ronnies' dialogue in *Star*

BUT FIRST THE NEWS

NICE TO BE WITH YOU AGAIN!

Peter Vincent

A STAR BOOK
published by
the Paperback Division of
W. H. ALLEN & Co Ltd

A Star Book
Published in 1977
by the Paperback Division of
W. H. Allen & Co. Ltd
A Howard and Wyndham Company
44 Hill St, London W1X 8LB

Copyright © Peter Vincent, 1977
Illustrations copyright © Graham Allen 1977
Cover photograph courtesy of Don Smith
This edition reprinted 1978

Printed in Great Britain by
Cox & Wyman Ltd, London, Reading and Fakenham

Typeset by Yale Press Ltd, London SE25

ISBN 0 352 30108 2

IN A
PACKED
SHOW TONIGHT...

RC:	Good evening. It's nice to be with you again, isn't it Ronnie?
RB:	Yes it is and in a packed show tonight we'll consider loneliness, with a special report from the Archbishop of Golders Green.
RC:	Then we'll look into complaints about the motor industry and we'll show you something that fell off the back of a lorry — it's the front of a lorry.
RB:	And we ask the searching question: Prince Rainier of Monaco — has he fallen from Grace?

1

RC:	And British deep sea divers with chicken pox — do they come up to scratch?
RB:	We take a look at the stormy marriage of an eskimo couple. It has lasted six months and they're wondering whether to call it a day.
RC:	Then a Scotsman will be telling us how to go skiing on only ten pounds — tie a five pound note to each foot.
RB:	We'll bring the latest news of the take-over of the Solomon Islands by cannibals — and we ask, will they cut off our coconuts?
RC:	For sports fans there'll be rugby with Eddie Waring, boxing with Eddie Tiring and archaeology with Eddie Downright-Boring.
RB:	And we'll be going over to the high jumping at the White City where the bar is already at seven foot three — so no one can get a drink.

3

RC: We'll also visit tonight's big charity ball in which well known personalities will be doing the things that have made them famous. Jimmy Tarbuck will be telling jokes, Pam Ayres will recite some poems, Uri Geller will ruin the cutlery and Christopher Lee will strangle a waiter.

RB: After that we'll talk to all seven members of the Dublin String Quartet.

RC: And to a masochist who likes nothing better than a cold bath every morning — so he has a warm bath every morning.

RB: And to a man who claims to be such a complete so-and-so that on Father's Day he sends a card addressed to *Anon*.

RC: And to a Scotsman who was very nearly drowned in the Black Sea while he was filling his fountain pen.

RB: And to a pathetic out-of-work contortionist who says he can no longer make ends meet.

RC:	Then we'll talk to a man who's found a cure for the common cold. Now he's trying to find a cure for the well-educated cold.
RB:	Then we talk to a really big noise in women's fashions: David Bowie.
RC:	And to an enormously tall boxer who's had to retire from the ring with cauliflower knees.
RB:	To the famous heiress who ran away with the milkman, was gone three months and came back three months gone.
RC:	And to farm labourer Fred Lurkin who fought for eighteen years to prevent a motorway being built through his kitchen — and won. Now they're building it through his living room.
RB:	Then we discuss government ministries — are there too many? We'll be hearing from the Minister of Steak and Kidney Pudding.

RC: Our film critic talks about
the new Danish sex
whodunnit
— apparently the butler was the
only one who didn't do it.

RB: Then a small man with a
dirty raincoat, from Zululand,
will tell us how he's sick of
always being picked out at
identity parades just because
his name is Asegai
Whadunme.

RC: Then we'll have some entertainment for you. First, Duncan McHoot, the well-known Scots drunkard, will play *Amazing Grace* on the breathalyser.

RB: Then we'll see another Scot, Jock McClog, a one-legged kilt dancer from the Gorbals, who specialises in high kicks and falling over.

RC: The Tooting Unmarried Mothers Operatic Society will be singing *Get me to the Church on Time*.

RB: Then we've got a rather
            unusual snake charming act
            featuring the world's most
            ancient performing reptiles.
            The act is called *Abdul and
            his Load of old Cobras.*

8

RC: And we're proud to feature the world's most short-sighted knife-thrower, Rudolpho Colenzo the Second and his assistant, Zelda the Twenty-ninth.

RB: And we'll end the entertainments with extracts from two rather daring plays, first, *Fanny by Gaslight*, then a new story about what goes on at the top of a fizzy lemonade factory, called *Gassy by Fanlight* and lastly the dramatic autobiography of an old lady who walked home across Hampstead Heath every evening in spite of many shifty men in dirty raincoats
— and that's called *Granny by Flashlight*.

We talked to a man who crossed...

RC:

Tonight we talk to a man who crossed a Gordon Highlander with a mousetrap and got a squeaky jockstrap.

RB:

And to a scientist from Kuwait who's bred an ostrich with a corkscrew head. You give it a fright and it drills for oil.

RC: Then we talk to a man who
        crossed a bulldog, a retriever
        and a scots terrier and got a
        very strong dog that tosses
        the caber and then brings it
        back.

RB: And to a man who crossed a
        field with Julie Andrews and
        got nothing at all.

RC: But we've just heard that the
        Noise Abatement Society and
        the Kennel Club have joined
        forces to produce Hush
        Puppies.

British scientists too made history this week in the field of interbreeding when they crossed a skunk with a fairy and got a whiffenpouf.

But We Had Hoped...

RC: But at this point we had
       hoped to interview the
       world's oldest man, but
       unfortunately he's had to cry
       off due to the unexpected
       illness of his father . . .

RB: — Who was injured playing
ice hockey on his honeymoon.
We had also hoped to
interview the Scottish
millionaire famous for
keeping all his money under
his mattress but this
morning he was injured in a
fall.
He fell off his bed to the floor
eighty feet below.

RC: We'd even hoped to show you the new easy way to fit a truss but the Producer wouldn't wear it.

RB: And we were going to have the dance group, The Five Foolish Virgins, but we've found out that two of them are really quite clever —

RC: And the other three are down with flu —

RB: But we *will* be telling you about a new BBC programme dealing with the problems of the oversexed. This programme will be shown fourteen times a week . . .

BUT FIRST— THE NEWS

RC: But first —
The News.
The Government announced today the new currency changes for the Common Market. The pound and the franc will join forces and become the prank; the mark will join the lira and become the lark; the gilder will join the pfennig and become the pfilder. There'll be ten pranks to the lark, six pfilders to the milder, five squarks to the splaark and a hundred dog ps in the dog pound.

RB: A sensational new plan was announced today to save money on the channel tunnel. As soon as it's built it'll be filled with water and we'll all be able to go through on the cross channel ferry.

RC: — Without getting wet. However the Captain of a transatlantic jumbo jet reported strong headwinds when he landed backwards in Tokyo this morning.

RB: In Uganda the President was asked today what he was going to do about tightening up defence. He replied, 'De fence? De man wid de nails am comin to fix it.'

RC: The President went on to say
        that he wished to return the
        twenty-six episodes of *Pot
        Black* that he had bought
        under the impression that it
        was a cooking programme.
RB: And he went on to announce
        that as an economy measure
        he has traded in his E type
        jaguar for an F type
        crocodile.

RC: British customs officials have arrested a famous Russian woman spy after the discovery of two miniature radios hidden in the cups of her bra. Said an official, 'We became suspicious when from the top of her dress we heard Kenneth McKellar singing, *The Hills are Alive with the Sound of Music.*'

RB: A Danish importer who lost a trunkful of highly pornographic books on the luggage escalator at London Airport has at last managed to find them. His trunk came up last Wednesday
— and his case comes up next Thursday.

RC: A beautiful young Swedish girl who'd gone swimming in the nude was rescued today by the crew of a Scottish trawler. To save her embarrassment they quickly covered her with an old macintosh
— Mr Angus Macintosh of Fyfe — who was delighted.

RB: We hear from the talks in Washington that an egg thrown by a demonstrator narrowly missed President Carter
— when it hit Mr Callaghan in the face.

RC: President Carter announced today that the U.S. space programme is so short of funds that in future all astronauts who go to the moon will have to pay their own fare.

RB: Meanwhile American astronauts have successfully landed on Mars. Here they encountered a native of the planet, a giant geranium with one huge eye and flippers like a seal. When they approached it, the geranium blinked its eye, flipped its flippers, burst into flames and perished. Luckily they managed to take a film of the blinking blooming flipping flaming perishing thing.

RC: And the Irish Space Agency announce that they have now invented a convertible capsule so their astronauts can ride with the top down if the weather's fine.

MEANWHILE IN BRITAIN...

RB: Meanwhile in Britain, the Prime Minister held a meeting with the Cabinet today. He also spoke to the bookcase and argued with the chest of drawers.

RC: But tomorrow the Prime Minister will receive a secret visit from Mr Brezhnev, according to informed sources in Moscow. Completely *un*informed sources stated: 'We don't know anything about it.'

RB: Whilst at the annual meeting of the Squatters' Association, the Minister of Housing gave his usual address. And fifteen members moved into it.

RC: Mrs Thatcher reminded the House of Commons today that before long this country would have a woman Prime Minister. Mr Edward Heath said, 'I heartily agree.' Mr Heath was wearing a powder blue dress with matching hat and accessories.

RB: Mrs Thatcher has just taken delivery of an open sports car. It is fitted with an up-to-the-minute extra to protect her hairdo. In the event of bad weather she only has to press a button and it stops raining.

RC: 'We are not yet out of the wood . . . It's going to be slow going . . .' said Mr Heath today from his yacht, fourteen miles from the Sussex coast. A crew member commented, 'It's hopeless trying to sail round East Grinstead.'

RB: It's reported that two eminent doctors who examined the ears of one of Britain's leading politicians are concerned about what they saw. They saw each other.

RC: In the House of Commons last night, when the heating failed, MPs had to don spare overalls to keep warm. Mr Callaghan wore four pairs whilst Mrs Thatcher wore three pairs, an overall majority of one.

RB: Government agricultural experts announce a revolutionary new insecticide. It kills all the crops so the insects starve to death.

RC: A Government survey on the labelling of toilet doors has just announced its findings. In most undertakers' the doors are labelled *His* and *Hearse*, in a Franciscan monastery the doors were labelled *Silent Order* and *Out of Order*, while the Civil Service has three doors marked *In*, *Out* and *Pending*.

RB: And important statistics are revealed today about why husbands get out of bed at night. It seems 5% get up with insomnia, 10% get up to go to the bathroom and 85% get up and go home.

RC: There was a record number of births in Kilburn this week. Apparently it was all due to the Irish Sweep. But he's now moved to Camden Town.

RB: Electricity reductions were so severe in London this evening that in the first race at Wembley Greyhound Stadium, the electric hare came third.

RC: And all the blue lamps turned to red, enabling Policewoman Charlotte Stallybrass to make three arrests
— and seven guineas.

RB: Fanny Cradock has announced that she's to join Women's Lib. When asked if she would be burning her bra she said, 'No darling, I'll sautée it with onions and a little white wine.'

RC: At London Zoo last night, Mr
and Mrs Horace Bungstrom
were accidentally locked in an
empty cage at closing time.
This is the first time that Mr
and Mrs Bungstrom have
mated in captivity.

RB: We've gleaned the following items of news by listening to two short-wave radio stations at once. We haven't had time to edit so here we go:

RC: The President of Caramba arrived in Britain today. He was —

RB: — wearing a fawn coloured
raincoat and had a scar over
his left ear. A lady explorer
just back from Ethiopia tells
how a few years ago she lost
all her clothes in a tropical
rainstorm. She then met an
important man and realised
to her embarrassment that he
was in fact, Haille —

RC: — delighted. The President of
the Newport Camden Family
Planning Association is to
have yet another child.

RB: — Anyone who saw the
accident is asked to phone
Scotland Yard, Whitehall
one —

RC: — Arsenal three. In the Miss World Competition today, Miss Sweden was placed first. A close second was —

RB: — Mr Michael Foot. The Commons then debated the price of syrup of figs but —

RC: — only three ran. In the Gloria van Crumpett divorce case the corespondent was named as —

RB: — The Argyll and Sutherland Highlanders with the help of the Highland Light Infantry.

RC:
But here's a special announcement. The Government is to levy V.A.T. on words. This means that a lot of words will have to be shorter. Now here's tomorrow's news:
The Quee and the Duk of Ed flew by conc last nig to visit Mr Cart. Meanwhile at Cow in the Is of Wig, Mr Ed Heat won the Cow yac race in his bra new yac. Lat footba res: Tott Hot two, Arse nil.

RB:
Here is a news flash just come in:
Milk bottles were thrown at a meeting of the Milk Marketing Board this afternoon and a meeting of the Egg Marketing Board was also broken up when eggs were thrown. A mass meeting of the Manure Marketing Board has been cancelled.

ABOUT THE WORKERS...

RC: Mr Reg Pringle, a worker at British Leyland, was presented today with a gold watch. He's been working at the company continously without any time off for illness for fifty minutes.

RB: A factory in Birmingham laid off 500 car body workers. They said, 'We can't find work for them. We only make digestive biscuits.'

RC: When the Prime Minister attended a rowdy workers' meeting at Longbridge today 90% of the workers applauded. However a union official commented afterwards that 10% of the workers were booing and the other 90% were applauding the booing.

RB: The Industrial Relations Board is investigating complaints about a works canteen in Solihull. Apparently the food is so bad the men are striking for shorter dinner breaks.

RC: While at a Birmingham factory this afternoon a man lost two fingers in an accident. He didn't actually notice the loss until he was saying goodnight to the foreman.

RB: We've just heard that due to the electricians strike, *Oh Calcutta!* is to be renamed *Fanny by Gaslight.*

RC: And the recent airline strike has meant that a Hampshire woman not only had to carry her luggage onto the plane but also had to finish her journey by rail. She claimed she left Hurn by plane for Albania and arrived at Albania by train with a hernia.

RB: But girl strippers in Old
Compton Street who've been
on strike accepted a motion
to return to work, after a
show of hands
— knees and bumpsidaisy.

RC:	A new electric car is to be withdrawn from the market. A spokesman said, 'It was a failure. It could only travel three yards as the flex wasn't long enough.'
RB:	But we've just had news of three important business mergers: Pye records have merged with Apple records to make Apple Pyes —
RC:	— B.A.C. have joined with Cyril Lord's to make flying carpets for the Persian market —
RB:	— And Krispie Bacon Limited have merged with Rolls Royce to make Sausage Rolls and Royce Krispies.
RC:	Owing to the shortage of free range chickens several government committees are to be set up to study new ways of hatching eggs. Mr Cyril Smith has promised he will sit on as many as he can.
RB:	Finally, a row developed today over Sussex County Council's new library catalogue for 1978. It lists the B.R. timetable under fiction.

The world of medicine

RC: Reports that British doctors are trying to specialise in too many branches of medicine were denied today by Doctor Cedric Milford, an ear, nose, throat, dandruff and belly button consultant.

RB: Britain's first pregnant man complained tonight about his treatment by the Press. He said, 'All this publicity makes me sick — especially in the mornings.'

RC: Doctors in a certain area of London are worried by the condition of Mr Ron Spriggs, a milkman from Putney who has appeared on ninety-three different census forms.

RB:

RC:

The Family Planning
Association announce that in
Britain, 90% of all parents
are, or have been, on the pill.
And 85% of them are women.
Of these 85%, 20% are now
on it and 13% are now off it,
12% are on it on and off and
9% are off it off and on, 8%
are often on it, 7% are often
off it, 6% are off it and wish
they were on it and 4% are
on it and off it so seldom it
doesn't matter. 3% are don't
knows, 2% are don't cares,
1% are no, don't!s and Mrs
Ivy Whizzer was disqualified
for ruining her entrance form.

RB: A man who swallowed a barometer was admitted to Cheadle Cottage Hospital tonight. His conditon was described as 'Set fair — stormy later.'

The Art World

RC: The Art World. The engagement was announced today between the famous post impressionist Madeleine Renoir and Mr Percy Edwards, the famous animal impersonator. They met when he was giving his impression of a dog and she was giving her impression of a post.

The Boston Bean ensemble is
to amalgamate with the
Boston Raddish Ensemble to
form the Boston Wind
Ensemble.

RC: When floodwater filled the Festival Hall last night, the seventeen stone contralto, Renata Lindstrom, escaped by floating through the doors on a double bass. She was accompanied by Donald Swann on the piano.

RB: And we've just heard that *Amazing Grace* has gone to number eight with Gladys Knight and The Pips at number nine. Mr Callaghan at number ten said 'It's ruining the tone of the neighbourhood.'

...OLOGISTS

RC:
The teeth of a prehistoric mammoth were found today in Sussex. This is a double event, according to the man who found them, Professor Hugh Stuckey. Not only are they the world's oldest teeth but they were found in the world's largest glass of water.

RB:
Archaeologists also report that the skeleton of a man, that suggests our ancestors were much taller than we are, was dug up today at East Acton ... West Acton and Ealing.

RC: And there's news of a South
       American tribe where the
       women make themselves
       attractive by covering their
       skins in mud, rotting brussels
       sprouts and linseed oil. The
       tribe is extinct.

RB: And the Zoological Society have just issued a new report on the mating of animals. Apparently ostriches mate once a week, crocodiles three times a week and elephants three weeks a time.

SOCIAL EVENTS

RC: In the beauty contest to find Miss Trawler of 1977 Miss Holland was found to be outside the limits, Miss Russian turned out to be a spy in disguise and Miss United Kingdom looked certain to win when Miss Iceland cut her gear.

RB: In the National Dance Festival at Finsbury this evening, the crowd became so excited, police had to link arms and hold them back. They were pushed forward four times but each time they struggled back again. The police were commended for their restraint and awarded first prize in the hokey cokey.

RC: The garden party at Buckingham Palace was a huge success. Thirty-three gardens attended along with seven cabbage patches and a rockery. But Percy Thrower's compost heap was refused admission.

RB: At the big Fancy Dress Ball
last night given by the
Football Pools Federation, a
young lady arrived entirely
naked except for a cross
marked on each bosom. She
was allowed in when she
explained that she was a
chest of draws.

RC: Short sighted Lady Myopia
       Fotheringay was in the news
       again when she opened the
       new haberdashery centre at
       Slough by cutting a
       ceremonial ribbon. As she did
       so, a large crowd cheered and
       her knickers fell down.

RB: The wedding took place in Pinewood today of Sylvia Lummox, for twenty-seven years a cinema usherette. The organist played selections from *The Sound of Music;* during the sermon the sidesman sold ice cream and the bride herself, all in white, came down the aisle backwards, waving a torch.

RC: But we've just heard that the world's most indecisive man was born today. He is forty-seven.

WEATHER

RC: Severe storms in the Western Approaches this afternoon ripped signal flags from ships of the Atlantic Fleet but they managed to get a message through with makeshift flags — and here it is: 'Weather absolutely underpants. Captain is in bed with a nasty red spotted handkerchief complicated by purple bloomers.'

RB: Temperatures. Here are the
lunchtime figures:
Birmingham twenty-two,
London twenty-one,
Manchester nineteen and
Liverpool twenty-three.
Liverpool go on to meet
Birmingham in the final.

Society Gossip

RC: The Annual General Meeting of the Claustrophobia Society at the Albert Hall was a fiasco. Only one member turned up and he kept shouting, 'Let me out!'

RB: And the President of the Sex Change Association, Mr Daphne Smith, is to marry Miss George Watson. Miss Watson, the former Mr Angela Watson will marry Mr Smith, the former Miss Henry Smith, at St John's Wood Registry Office, the former St Martha's Wood Registry Office.

RC: A new report from the Society of Perfect Printing states that 'British printing is food and getting butter every day. This is due to the fact that all the balley poofs get careful studs.'

RB: There's less good news from the National Conference of Henpecked Husbands at the South Norwood Astrodrome. The conference failed to turn up. It had to go and mow the lawn.

RC: Better news from the West Ham Short-Sighted Society. They held a picnic on Clapham Common ... And the East Ham Short-Sighted Society held a picnic on the West Ham Short-Sighted Society.

RB:	Today's anniversaries: Jimmy Tarbuck had a telegram from the Queen today. His jokes were exactly one hundred years old.
RC:	And shy spinster, Hester Pettigrew, was awarded the George Cross for saving the life of a drowning man. She gave him the kiss of life with her bicycle pump.
RB:	A soldier at Catterick was awarded the M.C. for saving a whole battalion of men. He shot the cook.

SPORTS NEWS

RC

Fulham F.C., worried by falling attendances, have just paid £90,000 for three spectators from Liverpool.

RB:

George Rumford, the Neasden Palace striker who committed a vicious foul in Saturday's televised game, was today awarded a six match suspension, four for the offence and two for the action replay.

RC: At the Ladies' Show Jumping, The Hon. Daphne Squire-Pilkington got three faults for a refusal — and Miss Elsie Jones got four pounds for an acceptance.

RB: In the Transatlantic single-handed yacht race Mr Owen Smithers has been disqualified for using both hands.

RC: Tonight's tug-of-war between England and France may have to be cancelled if nobody can find a twenty-six mile rope.

RB: Sir Hartley Withers, the explorer, had a fantastic escape today. He was being pursued along a river bank by three hungry lions, and just as it seemed they were certain to catch him, he was eaten by a crocodile.

RC: The goodwill tour of British sporting fixtures by Miss Racquel Welch has been causing certain embarrassments this week. Firstly—golf. At St Andrews Miss Welch had a hole in one ... and a very interesting split in the other.

RB: But champion jockey Ainsley Beasley was injured at Waverley today. He received a black eye when Racquel Welch turned round too quickly to say hello.

RC: And in the National Poker Championships at Olympia, the building was packed when the poker players heard that Raquel Welch and Elizabeth Taylor were outside — so everyone rushed out to see them. Which just proves that two pairs can beat a full house.

RB: Mountaineers using the new elastic rope on Kanchenjunga report one great advantage. If you do happen to slip you finish on a higher ledge than the one you fell from.

RC: The World Convention on Witch Doctors arrived at Heathrow today by Mumbo Jumbo jet —

RB: — They proceeded to the Albert Hall for the contest to decide which witch doctor could shrink his opponents to the smallest size in the shortest time. The match began on the platform, continued on a desk top and ended in a drawer.

RC: Whilst in the World Plumbing Championships in Oslo, the Dutch entry was flooded, the Icelandic entry froze, the Chinese entry was disqualified for flushing from right to left and the British entry said it would be round first thing in the morning.

RB: On the eve of the vital chess match against Russia, ths directors of the British Chess Federation have asked Cyril Smith to sit on the Board — but only if we're losing.

RC: In Belper, this evening, Mr Dudley Arkwright ate 622 radishes in six minutes twenty-three seconds. This doesn't count as a world record as he had a following wind.

NOW HERE ARE THE ANNOUNCEMENTS...

RB: Now here are the
        announcements. Police report
        exceptionally heavy traffic
        over Putney Bridge. It's been
        so heavy in fact that one
        woman had to abandon her
        car and continue her driving
        test on foot.

RC: A party from the Lazy Coach Drivers Society sets off today for a fortnight's tour of Victoria Coach Station.

RB: And the Ministry of Transport announce a new roundabout on the A1. It's 10p a go, three minutes a ride. Bring the children.

RC: The Ministry also announce a new scheme to solve the traffic problems on roads leading to the West Country. There's to be a special lane for traffic jams.

RB: And here is a police message for Mr and Mrs Smith, believed to be spending the weekend in Brighton. Will Mr Smith please return to his home in Chorley where his wife, Mrs Jackson, is absolutely furious.

RC: The Gay Lib recruiting
            vehicle may be touring your
            area this week. It's easy to
            recognize. It's mauve in
            colour and the number plate
            is RU 1-2.

RB: We've just been handed an
            urgent warning about
            Trimmet's Treacle Puddings,
            which have caused several
            people to be sent to hospital
            with badly scalded feet. It
            seems people have
            misunderstood the
            instructions which read,
            'Before opening tin, stand in
            boiling water for twenty
            minutes.'

RC: The South Pilling Fire
            Brigade which has been late
            for every fire in the last
            seven years is seeking
            suggestions as to what can
            be going wrong. If you've
            any ideas please ring the Fire
            Brigade at South Pilling
            67421865992487164 —
            Extension 7787124
            — and leave a message on
            the answer phone.

RB:	The Convention of Irish Wizards announce that due to the drought a rainmaking ceremony will be held in Phoenix Park, Dublin, or if wet, in the City Hall.
RC:	After our beauty advice last week a young lady has written to us about her worried frown and overdeveloped bust — but we advise her to grin and bear it.
RB:	We've been asked by the Health Service to explain the use of the hospital bell. In fact you should ring it once if you need anything, twice if it's urgent and three times if it's too late.
RC:	And we've advice for the ladies. If your electric blanket doesn't work, switch it off at once and call in a man.
RB:	Here is a message for seven honeymoon couples in a hotel in Peebles: breakfast was served three days ago.

RC:	Good news for peeping Toms. The lady who runs the famous Aunt Maud advice column has agreed to help them . . . she's going to leave her bedroom curtains open on Thursdays.
RB:	The B.M.A. has asked us to give a simple piece of advice to men who wish to avoid falling hair. Get out of the way.
RC:	We must apologize for a fault in today's farming programme, *Compost for Beginners.* Vision and sound have failed. The programme will continue in smell only.
RB:	But here's an important BBC message for long wave listeners: you can stop waving now.
RC:	Lastly we have to apologize for an earlier butlletin concerning a prisoner who escaped from a South African gaol. We should have said he was a trusty prisoner who escaped in The Rand — not a randy prisoner who escaped in a truss.

Thats Entertainment

RB: There was a crisis in a circus at Bletchley today when the lion escaped and threw the whole place into a panic. The strongest man in the world fainted and the indiarubber man completely erased the tattooed lady.

RC: And we've just heard that Raquel Welch has been signed to play Quasimodo in a new film entitled *The Hunchfront of Notre Dame.*

LATE
WEATHER
NEWS

RB: There's a wonderful weather forecast for tomorrow. It's going to be seventy degrees — twenty in the morning, thirty at midday and twenty in the evening.

RC: Reports are coming in of a freak tidal wave in Birmingham, mountain avalanches in Norfolk, six-foot snowdrifts in the North Sea and a very good party at the Met Office.

And now a sketch...

RB: And now a sketch about
         enormous embarrassments at
         a small intimate party.
         Ronnie Corbett will play the
         small intimate party and I
         will play the enormous
         embarrassments.

BUT WE'VE JUST HEARD...

Crime

RC: From the world of crime we've just heard that the series of thefts from cabinet ministers still goes on. Tonight we talk to the Minister without Portfolio, the Minister without a Bicycle and the Minister without Trousers.

RB: Reports are also coming in of
        a big jewel raid said to have
        been committed by Sooty.
        Harry Corbett is believed to
        have had a hand in it.

RC: A man was charged today with eccentric behaviour in certain London streets. He went to Pudding Lane and made a pudding for himself, he went to Gooseberry Lane and made a fool of himself, then he went to Exhibiton Road and got himself arrested.

RB: Mr Lemuel Shift, described as the world's sneakiest little man, denied today that he'd been to Scotland Yard to take a lie detector test. If there was one missing, he said, it was nothing to do with him.

RC: A man who was caught peeking into the changing cubicles at an outsize woman's dress shop described himself as a quantity surveyor.

RB: And at a certain church in Hertfordshire both the Vicar and his housekeeper have been suspended. They found his vest in her pantry and her pants in his vestry.

Temperance Toyshops are to withdraw a thousand-piece nude jigsaw of Tom Jones unless seventy-three pieces are withdrawn.

Police Ten

RB,   A man in Hexham telephoned the police today to say his house had been burgled by a raving lunatic. When asked how he knew it was a raving lunatic, he said, 'because he took nothing of value, only my wife.'

RC: And a thief broke into a men's outfitters in London. He stole only a truss and a straw boater. Police are looking for a *very* careful tap dancer.

RB: A chemist's shop in Eastbourne was broken into last night. The entire stock was taken except for quantities of hair cream and the pill. Police are looking for a bald headed Catholic.

RC: A man who blindfolds policemen and steals their spectacles struck again in Ashbourne this evening. Police are vaguely groping for a tall man with a smelly suit.

RB: Whilst at Pirbright Police Station a woman claimed that a squad of cavalrymen from the Light Brigade crept up to her house and seduced her. When asked if she would prefer charges she replied, 'Yes I would. It would be noisy but I wouldn't be kept waiting so long . . .'

RC: But now a message from the
        police in Finchley. They say
        that of the two rabbits stolen
        last week from Peter's
        Petshop, only fourteen have
        so far been recovered.

P.B: The grave of Sir Cheevely Robley, the jam tycoon, was opened by police today. On the lid of the coffin they found the words, 'To open, pierce with a pin and prise lid off with a penny'.

RC: More than one hundred policemen, searching for stolen jewellery, dragged Staines reservoir for three hours. They dragged it as far as the River Thames where it fell in.

RB:	There was a fracas in London in the small hours of this morning, involving a Seamus O'Higgins. After a lengthy argument O'Higgins was arrested by P.C. Wallace Grudgeon who claimed his nose was broken in three places — Marble Arch, Piccadilly Circus and Tower Bridge.
RC:	And thieves in a stolen car were apprehended after a 100 mph chase by P.C. Wainwright who followed them on foot. Said. P.C. Wainwright, afterwards, 'I had no choice. They shut the door on my truncheon.'

And Three From Ireland...

RB: Police broke into the home of
        Ireland's most brilliant forger
        today and took away two
        million seven-pound notes.

RC: When a clever gang of
        thieves were caught red
        handed in a Dublin bank
        police immediately sealed all
        the exits
        — so the gang escaped
        through all the entrances.

RB: But two Irishmen were apprehended when they broke into a Dublin bookmakers and lost £800. The two men charged were Terrence Finnegan who gave his address as *no fixed abode* and Paddy Muldoon who, when asked for his address said, 'I live in the flat above him.'

Today in the courts...

RC: Today in the courts an unemployed labourer was found guilty of running up and down Downing St at two o'clock in the morning shouting 'All the Government is barmy!' He was given a two pound fine for being drunk and disorderly and a ten-year gaol sentence for revealing a state secret.

RB: Mr Joseph Murk, the deep
sea diver who's campaigning
for more rest breaks and
shorter dives, and who threw
a jellyfish at the Minister for
the Environment, has been
sent down for three years.

RC: A journalist who slandered
the Chancellor of the
Exchequer very badly was
given a chance to do better in
the High Court today.

RB: While in the Central Criminal
        Court a man was acquitted of
        gross indecency as he'd only
        been indecent 143 times.
RC: Mr Henry Gummage, the
        farm labourer who suffered a
        serious injury from a reaping
        machine while dallying in the
        corn with a young lady, has
        successfully defended against
        three paternity suits on the
        grounds of diminished
        responsibility.

RB: In another court, a tailor's apprentice from Pusely complained that when he proposed to a short-sighted seamstress she not only turned him down but also trimmed his edges and sewed up his sides.

RC: And at the Old Bailey, Jim Spraggs, the world's greatest confidence trickster, sentenced the Judge to five years' hard labour.

RB: An insurance company refused to pay out a claim, stating that the claimant, Mr Henry Bowker, was blind drunk and smoking in bed. Mr Bowker won his case when he replied, 'I was not in the least drunk and anyway the bed was alight when I got into it.'

RC: At Bow St Magistrates Court, a man found guilty of stealing two thousand monopoly sets was ordered to go to gaol, go directly to gaol, not to pass *Go* and not to collect £200.

RB: A man who ate scampi
contaminated with mercury
successfully sued the Alpha
Bottled Scampi Co. for
injuries. He said every time
the temperature went up he
hit his head on the ceiling.

RC: Finally, a man complained of the noise made by the amorous couple in the flat above him. Each evening they'd sing *The Red Flag,* eat their supper, have fun on the sofa and take a very naughty bath together —

RB: — So every night it was hammer and sickle, cheese and pickle, slap and tickle and bubble and squeak.

IN THE DIVORCE COURT TODAY...

RC: In the divorce court today a husband claimed that his wife's mother kept shouting at him that he was driving too fast along the M1 — and to make matters worse she swore at him while he was untying her from the roof-rack.

RB: And an executive from a toothpaste manufacturing company was divorced by his wife on the grounds of cruelty. She claimed he kept squeezing her the wrong end.

RC: Then Madame Fifi Dubonnet, the former Picasso model, claimed that last Sunday her husband severely assaulted her and gave her three black eyes.

RB: But a sex-crazed lady
dietician from Welwyn
Garden City admitted in
court — 'Yes, there are 263
men in my life . . . and they
all eat shredded wheat . . .'

RC: In the next case a husband
claimed that he had seen the
milkman put his arm round
his wife three times.
Dismissing the case the
Judge said no milkman had
an arm that long.

RB: And a Mr George Thomas
was granted a divorce on the
grounds of his wife's
adultery. After the hearing
he stated, 'She led me a dog's
life. I was fed on scraps,
made to fetch slippers and
forced to beg for my
favourite biscuits. So when I
found her in bed with the
postman, I did what anyone
else in my position would
have done
— I bit him in the leg.'

RC: In an adjacent court Sheikh Haroun el Ramn is being sued for divorce by his 500 wives. It seems they came home early one night last week and caught him with 500 other women.

RB: In one case that finished, the world's greatest jigsaw designer was divorced after his wife found he was keeping a piece on the side.

RC: Later, three men who had failed to keep up with their alimony payments were repossessed by their ex-wives.

IN THE SKETCH THAT FOLLOWS...

RB: In the sketch that follows, which has been carefully cast by our new Irish producer, I play the part of Ronnie Corbett . . .

Well that's all for this week. Next week...

RC: Well, that's all for this week. Next week in *Stars On Sunday* Lester Piggott will read the sermon on the mount.

RB: But in another packed programme we'll be talking to Albert Nudge, a retired goldfish breeder, who's been appointed head of a committee to solve the pollution problem in the English Channel. He's already told the Government that they'll have to see that the water's changed three times a week.

RC: Then, in our new series, *Do It Yourself,* we'll be talking to a Mr Peter Robinson, the father and mother of three children.

RB: And we'll be talking to a generous Scotsman who once every year takes all his money out of the bank for a holiday
— and then, when it's had a holiday, he puts it all back again.

RC: Then we'll be talking to a man who's such a puritan he won't speak to his wife because she's a married woman.

RB:	Next we interview three Indian princes, the Mufti of Baroda, the Lounge Suit of Hyderabad and the Bedsock of Bangalore.
RC:	And we'll have a talk on Ethics — by a man from Thuthex.
RB:	Attractive Olga Follanova will discuss the sex lives of three great Russians, Boris Godanov, Boris Not-Quite-Godanov, and Boris Absolutely-Useless.
RC:	Then the interviews — we'll talk to a man who's really got a finger in every pie — he's a short sighted butcher.

RB: And to another great Irish forger who is able to take a fifty penny piece and file off the corners so accurately that he can pass it off as a ten penny piece.

RC: Then we'll ask some
               searching questions, like:
               education — can cross eyed
               teachers control their pupils?

RB: And we'll ask the cast of *Oh Calcutta!* to change roles as they all know each other's parts backwards.

RC: Which will lead us to discuss three famous oriental sex books, the Kama Sutra, the Less Calm Sutra and the Absolutely Frantic Sutra.

RB: Then by way of light relief we'll be taking a look at fur-covered toilet seats and asking: do they tickle your fancy?

RC: We'll show you the new Mafia scarecrow. It's so terrifying, not only do the birds not take any seeds, they bring back the seeds they took last year . . .

RB: We'll have a commentary on the launching of the Irish moon rocket — if they can find a bottle big enough to take the stick.

RC: Then in our series, *Great
          Optimists of Our Time,* we'll
          visit the Royal Hospital for
          Chelsea Pensioners and talk
          to the man who designed the
          maternity wing.

RB: In our celebrity interviews,
          Basil Brush will tell us where
          he gets his brushes, Wilfred
          Pickles will tell us where he
          gets his pickles and Simon
          Oates probably won't say
          anything.

RC:	As light relief, veteran fan dancer Mimi La Zouche will perform *The Dance of the Virgin* entirely from memory.
RB:	Then we'll feature the famous colour-blind poet, Mr Reginald Smithers. Here's an excerpt from one of his lovely poems:
RC:	*Roses are red,* *Violets are brown,* *The sky is bright yellow,* *And so are bluetits.*
RB:	This will be followed by a demonstration of sixteen ways of cooking sennapods by the Galloping Gourmet.

RC: Finally we'll show excerpts from Favourite BBC programmes, firstly from the classic, *Colditz Story,* then from the famous documentary about miners, *The Coal Tips Story,* and then from a new film starring Raquel Welch as an eskimo — which as yet has no title.

The End

Graham Allen.

RB: Well, that's the end of another series, now we go our separate ways. Ronnie Corbett will be appearing in *The Two Gentlemen of Verona* at the public baths in Looe and I'll be appearing in *The Two Public Looes of Verona* in the Gentlemen's at Bath.

RC: And that's all we've got room for in this book, isn't it, Ronnie?

RB: Yes it is and that means it's

RC:	Goodnight from me —
RB:	And it's goodnight from him.
BOTH:	Goodnight.

Wyndham Books are obtainable from many booksellers and newsagents. If you have any difficulty please send purchase price plus postage on the scale below to:

Wyndham Cash Sales,
44 Hill Street,
London W1X 8LB

OR

Star Book Service,
G.P.O. Box 29,
Douglas,
Isle of Man,
British Isles.

While every effort is made to keep prices low, it is sometimes necessary to increase prices at short notice. Wyndham Books reserve the right to show new retail prices on covers which may differ from those advertised in the text or elsewhere.

Postage and Packing Rate

U.K. & Eire
One book 15p plus 7p per copy for each additional book ordered to a maximum charge of 57p.

These charges are subject to Post Office charge fluctuations.